Only Horse People...

A look at a sport for the deranged!

Written & illustrated by Pam Stone

Published by Horse Hollow Press, Inc.

Made completely in the U.S.A.

Please note: While the author, Pam Stone, is not wearing a helmet on the back cover of this
book, we, at Horse Hollow Press, are proponents of wearing helmets and advise everyone to
wear one while riding, even if they are only doing flat work.

First printing: November 2005

ISBN: 0-9638814-9-3
Library of Congress Number: 2005932535

A Special Thanks

A special thanks to all the horses and instructors who taught me that the daily journey of training is worth far more than a wall full of ribbons. To my mother, Joan, for her artistic genes. To all the hysterical contributions from *Only Horse People* fans and especially for Paul, for his infinite patience and his willingness to 'muck in' whenever necessary...

A Note to our Readers

Writing and illustrating *Only Horse People* was a blast, and I was overwhelmed by contributions that came in from all over the U. S. and Canada. What I was not expecting is how frequently I received the same idea from several different people! Obviously, many of us are not alone in our *Only Horse People* experiences! Because of the limited amount of space on each page, I was forced to give credit to the first person (and horse) who had submitted a particular idea. Also, I received some wonderfully funny ideas after press. So, if you don't see your idea in this particular book, fear not, you may be included in the very next edition of *Only Horse People!*

Only Horse People are delighted by things that would disgust normal people.

Only Horse People display countless photos of their horse and only one of their spouse.

Only Horse People have
green "slime" stains
on every shirt they own.

Only Horse People would know why
a thermometer has a yard of yarn
tied to the end of it.

(Thanks to Vicki Little, Raisa and Curry)

Only Horse People can magically lower their voices five octaves to bellow at a pawing horse.

Only Horse People will spend 20 *minutes*
grooming their horse and
20 *seconds* grooming themselves.

(Thanks to Cj Wilson, Lady, Swifty Sweety and Prince)

Only Horse People think nothing of eating a sandwich after mucking stalls.

(Thanks to Katherine Walcott)

Only Horse People are oblivious when a horse "breaks wind."

Only Horse People would fail
to associate whips, chains
and leather with sexual deviancy.

(Thanks to Margie Lynn Loeser, Navarre and Polo)

Only Horse People can do relatively well regardless of their shape or size.

Only Horse People consider themselves
lucky if all they've ever broken
are fingers and toes.

(Thanks to Barbara Carry and Rampage)

Only Horse People can gross out an entire dinner party by discussing the more delicate areas of grooming.

Only Horse People never give up.

Only Horse People will take bandage scissors
to their hair when they find it
doesn't fit under their hard hat.

(Thanks to Katherine Walcott)

Only Horse People are banned from laundromats.

Only Horse People have a language
all their own.

(Thanks to Melissa Creswick and Signature)

Only Horse People, who are completely
unorganized and always late,
manage to be ready to enter at
'A' at precisely 9:23am.

(Thanks to Vicki Little, Raisa and Curry)

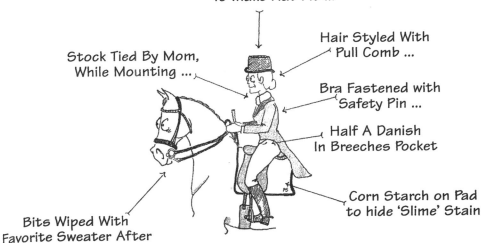

Gym Sock Wadded Inside
To Make Hat Fit ...

Hair Styled With
Pull Comb ...

Stock Tied By Mom,
While Mounting ...

Bra Fastened with
Safety Pin ...

Half A Danish
In Breeches Pocket

Corn Starch on Pad
to hide 'Slime' Stain

Bits Wiped With
Favorite Sweater After
Losing Towel ...

Only Horse People will
end relationships over their hobby.

Only Horse People know their financial priorities.

Only Horse People unknowingly demonstrate the same kind of affection on their mates as they do their pets.

Only Horse People cluck to their cars
to help them up the hills.

Only Horse People know it's impossible
to be in the same hemisphere
with a horse and stay clean.

Only Horse People insure their horses
for more than their cars.

(Thanks to Barbara Carry and Ms. America)

Only Horse People will give you
twenty names and reasons for
that bump on your horse.

(Thanks to Barbara Carry and Dutch Vivacious)

Only Horse People believe in
the 11th Commandment:
Inside leg to outside rein.

(Thanks to Vicki Little, Raisa and Curry)

Only Horse People think they can
stand in front of someone else's runaway
and actually make it stop.

(Thanks to Gloria Lonsdale and Moonshadow's Dream)

Only Horse People arrive at gala events in inappropriate vehicles.

(Thanks to Katy House and Percy)

Only Horse People will spend
hundreds of dollars over
a weekend for a 95¢ ribbon.

Only Horse People know more
about their horse's nutrition
than their own.

Only Horse People can be on
a week-long "high" after a good ride.

Only Horse People will sacrifice
their own health for that
of their horse's.

(Thanks to Stephanie Strong and Damon)

Only Horse People check out
the truck and trailer hitch first
before checking out the driver.

(Thanks to Melissa Creswick and Signature)

Only Horse People are married
to the most patient spouses on Earth.

Only Horse People think it's normal
to pick off ticks in public
after a long trail ride.

(Thanks to Kim Fuess)

Only Horse People are so trendy
that they all own the same kind of dog.

Only Horse People scream while emptying their bladders after a particularly "chafing" ride.

Only Horse People know that all topical medications come in either indelible blue or neon yellow.

(Thanks to Gayle Brodie)

Only Horse People love
receiving practical gifts.

Only Horse People will engage
in the same fruitless activity
day after day.

(Thanks to Karen Stansbury and Chinook)

Only Horse People will spend their last dime
on a "really neat two-year-old that
I just know I can turn around
and sell for ten grand!"

Only Horse People have oil stains on the carpet right next to the TV.

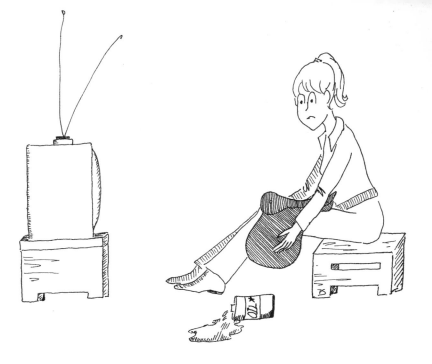

Only Horse People think they can succeed where all others have failed.

Only Horse People refuse to take vacations.

Only Horse People have strange, callused patches of "turkey skin" on their butts.

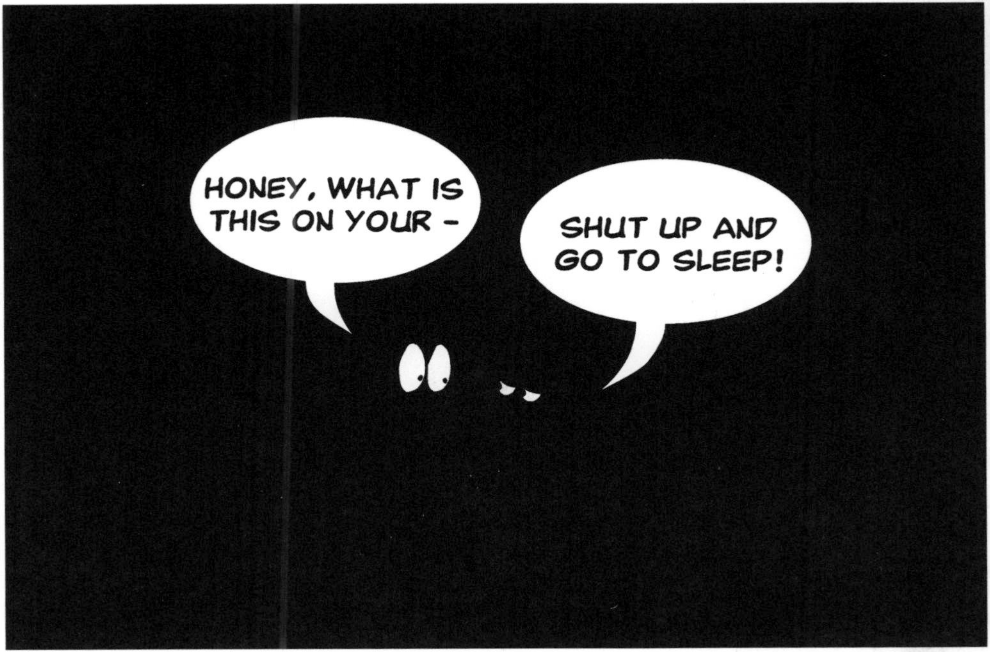
HONEY, WHAT IS THIS ON YOUR -
SHUT UP AND GO TO SLEEP!

Only Horse People have nice, year-round "tans."

Only Horse People have a vocabulary
that can make a sailor blush.

Only Horse People will argue about anything with anyone — except their trainer.

(Thanks to Margie Loeser, Navarre and Polo)

Only Horse People have less
of a wardrobe than their horse.

Only Horse People will spend good money to be verbally humiliated in public.

Only Horse People engage in a hobby that's more work than their day job.

Only Horse People do
so much for so little.

Only Horse People know
it's always their fault.

Hay there!

Want to be included in the next edition of *Only Horse People*? Just mail us your favorite *Only Horse People* experience. If included, you and your horse will receive on-page credit and Horse Hollow Press will send you a free copy of the book! In the case of duplications, we will credit the person who submitted the idea first.

www.pamstoneshow.com
Or mail to:
Pam Stone
c/o Horse Hollow Press, Inc.
PO Box 456
Goshen, NY 10924
www.horsehollowpress.com
info@horsehollowpress.com

Order more copies!

To order, photocopy this page and mail it to the address below or save freight and stop by your local tack or feed store to pick up a copy.

Yes! I want to order more books. Please send me:
Qty:

____ **Only Horse People** by Pam Stone. $9.95
____ **Anyone Can Draw Horses**. Teaches anyone to draw horses. $7.95
____ **It's All About Breakthroughs**. Natural horseman's guide. $16.95
____ **Trickonometry**: The Secrets of Teaching Your Horse Tricks. $23.9
____ **The Original Book of Horse Treats**. Recipes for treats. $19.95
____ **The Ultimate Guide to Pampering Your Horse**. Care tips. $24.95
____ **The Incredible Little Book of 10,001 Names for Horses**. $8.95
____ **The Wonderful Life of Lola**. Activity book. $4.95

Add $4.95 shipping and packing per order. Pay only one price for shipping, no matter how many books you order. **TOTAL ENCLOSED $**_____. (NY residents add sales tax.)

Mail to: Horse Hollow Press, Inc., PO Box 456, Goshen, NY 10924. (Include your name, address and phone.) Or call: 800-414-6773 to order. Credit cards accepted.